Wind Power

David Neufeld

Table of Contents

What Is Wind?

*S*omewhere on Earth the wind is blowing. The earth is a big wind generator driven by the sun. As the sun warms the earth, it heats the air above the land and water. The warm air rises and cool air flows in underneath. That's wind.

Wind can blow your roof off, cool you on a hot night, and pile sand into tall dunes. For centuries, people have tried to harness the enormous power of wind. They have used wind to move boats, to fly, and to generate electricity.

The energy of wind is **renewable**. Energy that is renewable will never run out.

Wind is a tremendous natural resource. Wind has the power to shape the land. It also has the power to help run our high-tech world.

Sailing with the Wind

Many thousands of years ago, somebody discovered that a good steady wind could save a lot of paddling. A fair wind could take a boat where sailors wanted to go.

Maybe the discovery went like this:

A group of people had a raft. They wanted to travel to a nearby island. They knew that the wind came up and blew toward the island every afternoon.

This raft was built to look like an ancient sailing raft. It was sailed across the Pacific Ocean to re-create early sea voyages.

They brought a pole with a crosspiece and put it in the boat. Attached to the crosspiece was a piece of square cloth. They pushed off from the beach. The breeze came up behind them. Up went the pole and crosspiece. The sailors held onto the bottom corners of the sail and felt the tug of the wind. The boat picked up speed but squirmed around. A person in the back of the boat stuck a paddle in the water and used it to steer. They sat back and grinned and let the wind do the work. They were sailing!

That's one possible explanation of the first sailing trip. No one knows who invented the first sailboats, but historians have found illustrations and paintings of boats from ancient times. There are records of ancient Egyptians using simple sailboats on the Nile River and Pacific Islanders sailing the South Pacific many thousands of years ago.

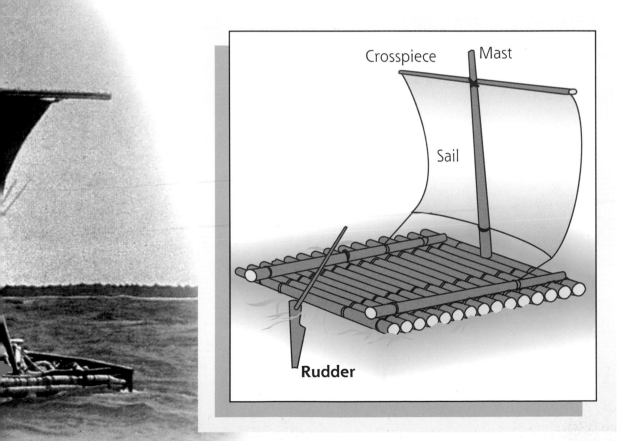

Trade Winds

Wind is a current of air. Because of the way the earth is heated and the way it rotates, warm air is always flowing to the equator. These currents of air are called the trade winds. Sailors used these winds to get where they wanted to go.

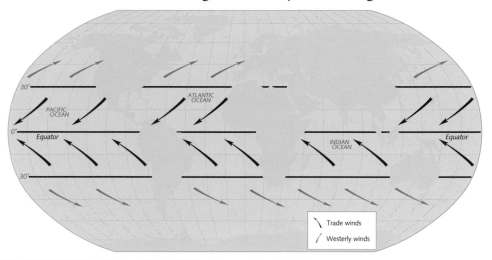

Exploring the World

After people learned how to sail, some bold and curious ones set out to explore the world. Early sailboats traveled with wind behind them pushing their boats. The wind pushed the sailboats in the direction it was blowing. Sailors watched for winds that were blowing where they wanted to go.

As early as the late 1400s, sailors were setting out from Europe for North America or in search of sea routes to Asia. They discovered that there were steady winds blowing in the direction they wanted to sail—from east to west. They called these winds **trade winds** because they hoped the winds would provide them with an ocean route for trading goods with people in other parts of the world.

While the trade winds gave sailors a reliable way to cross the oceans, people still worked hard to create faster ships. Clipper ships first appeared during the 1800s. With three **masts** and more than a dozen sails, clipper ships were the most awesome wind machines ever built. The massive sails caught the wind and made the huge ships sail at a fast clip.

Clipper ships were used to carry **goods** such as tea, wool, and silk from one country to another. They could carry more than 4,000 tons of goods. A ship arriving first in a **port** could get the best price for the tea and other goods on board. So clipper ships raced each other from one part of the world to another.

In 1849, one of the first clipper ships sailed from China to New York in a record-breaking 74 days and 14 hours. It took some ships a year to make the same trip.

Sailing Through History

As sailors learned more about the wind, they built boats with different kinds of sails to help them travel from place to place.

Chinese junk
Ancient times to present
The Chinese junk has sails made of linen or bamboo, which can be raised and lowered like a venetian blind.

Arab dhow
700s to present
Turks, Egyptians, Persians, and other groups sailed these ships through the Indian Ocean. They used them for trading spices, silks, and other goods.

Viking long ship
800s to 1100s
Viking explorers sailed through the North Atlantic in these narrow boats, which had just one sail.

Caravel
1400s to 1600s
Christopher Columbus, Vasco da Gama, and other famous explorers used these ships, which had two to four masts, on their voyages.

Spanish galleon
1400s to 1600s
The Spanish galleon had at least three masts and square sails. It usually had two or more decks. The Spanish used this ship for trading goods and also as a warship.

Clipper ship
1800s
The clipper ship had a sharp **bow**, many sails, tall masts, and was built for great speed. Clipper ships were used for trade.

People from many countries still go sailing today. They sail for fun and for sport.

For thousands of years, sailors went to sea in ships powered by the wind. These sailing ships carried explorers around the globe, brought settlers to new countries, and let people trade goods around the world.

Then shipbuilders began using engines to power their ships. The American inventor Robert Fulton designed the first steam engine-powered ship, the *Clermont*, which sailed up the Hudson River from New York City to Albany in 1807. Soon all cargo ships had steam engines. Cargo ships today are powered with oil. And sailboats are now used mainly for sport.

Flying with the Wind

At the same time people were discovering how wind could carry boats across the water, they were also discovering how to use the power of wind to carry things into the air.

Kites were the first objects successfully flown in the sky. The first kites were probably invented in China about 3,000 years ago and were made of bamboo and silk.

A kite acts like a big sail. A person runs along with a kite until the wind catches it and lifts it into the air. The wind keeps the kite flying.

The Chinese dragon kite, which can be from 18 to 30 meters long, is flown at festivals and New Year's celebrations.

From the start, people found different ways to use kites. A general in China flew a kite from his camp to his enemy's palace and used the string to measure the distance between the two places. Workers building towers in Japan used kites to help raise bricks and other supplies to the top of the tower.

Scientists also used kites to study the wind and weather. In the 1700s, two scientists used kites to measure the temperature at different **altitudes**. They flew kites with thermometers tied at different levels on the kites' strings. Benjamin Franklin conducted what might be the most famous kite experiment ever. He flew a kite during a lightning storm to prove that lightning was a form of electricity.

People also tried to use kites—and the wind—to carry or move people. In 1827, an inventor in England created a carriage that was moved by kites. In 1903, Samuel Franklin Cody crossed the English Channel on a boat that was pulled by kites.

Today, people fly kites for fun.

Gulls and other birds glide on **air currents.** Sometimes a bird rides the current for a long time without flapping its wings or losing altitude. People watched birds and wondered if they could do the same.

Gliders

It's no surprise that as people were launching kites into flight, they were also thinking about how to launch a person into flight. For thousands of years, people watched birds and wanted to fly like them. Birds seemed to have the secrets of using the wind to travel through the air. Many people tried to build wings and imitate the flight of birds. Some of them got off the ground, but none stayed up in the air for long.

Then in Germany in the late 1800s, Otto Lilienthal, an **engineer**, began to experiment with **gliders**. He built his glider by stretching canvas over a lightweight frame made of willow branches. In the center of the glider, there was a harness to hold the pilot.

Lilienthal built a hill to launch his gliders. He ran down his hill into the wind until he lifted off. Otto completed almost 2,000 successful short flights, but he had many crashes as well.

Lilienthal's experiments with gliders taught him about **aerodynamics**, or how the shape of an object affects how it flies through the air. He discovered what wing shapes and designs would be best able to catch the wind and lift the glider into flight.

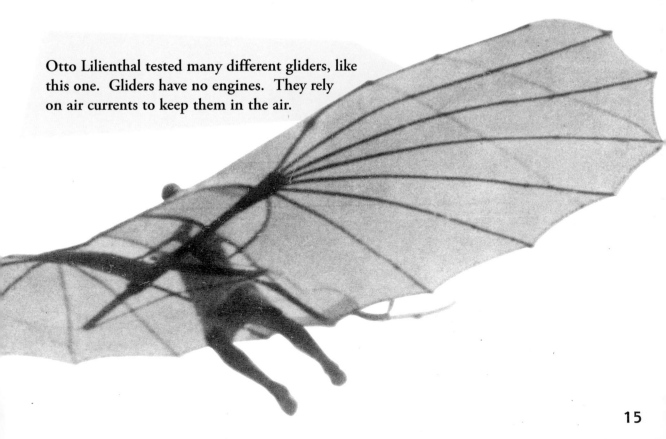

Otto Lilienthal tested many different gliders, like this one. Gliders have no engines. They rely on air currents to keep them in the air.

Orville and Wilbur Wright launch their glider at Kitty Hawk, North Carolina. The Wright brothers' 1902 glider led the way for the first airplane flight in 1903.

The Wright Brothers

Wilbur and Orville Wright read about Lilienthal's work. The Wright brothers experimented further with gliders in order to learn about using air currents to fly. What they learned helped them to build their first engine-powered plane.

The Wright brothers wrote to the United States Weather Bureau to find a place with steady winds where they could test their gliders. The sand dunes on the Outer Banks near Kitty Hawk, North Carolina, were perfect. The Outer Banks often have winds of 10 to 20 miles per hour. The dunes provided soft sand to land on.

One perfect day, Orville and a local man, Dan Tate, launched Wilbur from a sand dune. They ran down the dune holding the glider's wingtips. When they let go, Wilbur and the glider flew gracefully for 15 or 20 seconds.

The following year, Wilbur tried to turn the glider by bending

the wings. The glider spun and crashed, and Wilbur got cuts and a black eye. Nobody had ever made a glider turn in the air.

That winter, the Wright brothers built a **wind tunnel** in their bicycle shop back home in Ohio. The wind tunnel was a wooden, rectangular box with a fan at one end and an opening at the other. They built small model gliders with more than 200 different wing designs and tested them by flying them through the wind tunnel.

The Wright brothers also flew gliders like kites—without a pilot. This let them test different wing structures in different wind conditions—and let them avoid a few crash landings.

The glider that the Wright brothers built in 1902 was a breakthrough. The new design allowed the pilot to turn the glider in flight. What Wilbur and Orville Wright discovered about the shape and design of glider and airplane wings is still used on every aircraft built today.

Gliders Today

Today, airplanes have engines that propel them through the air, but people still like to hang glide as a sport. Hang gliding gives people a chance to soar through the air like a bird.

Modern hang gliders have wings made of nylon or other light, sturdy fabrics. The pilot is strapped into a lightweight metal frame that hangs from the wings. The method of taking off hasn't changed much in the last hundred years. Just like Otto Lilienthal and the Wright brothers, hang-glider pilots still take off from a high point and still look for a soft place to land. Often they will hike up steep mountains so they can soar down from the mountaintop.

Hang gliding is safer today, but glider pilots need expert training and special equipment. There are schools that teach people how to hang glide.

A skilled glider pilot, who understands the wind, can keep a glider plane in the air for hours.

Once in flight, pilots can control their height and direction by adjusting their body positions and the control bar that is attached to the wings.

People also fly engineless planes called glider planes, or sailplanes. These planes are towed about 600 meters up into the air by a propeller plane and then let loose. The glider plane is able to fly using the air currents.

Before a person went up in the Montgolfier balloon, the inventors sent a duck, a sheep, and a rooster up in the balloon to prove that living things could stay alive in the sky.

Balloons

Gliders aren't the only way to travel with the wind. For more than 200 years, people have flown in balloons as well. Balloons rise when they are filled with hot air or gases that are lighter than air, such as hydrogen or helium. Then they move according to the direction of the wind.

In 1783, two Frenchmen made the world's first successful balloon flight. They flew in a balloon that was created by the Montgolfier brothers. The balloon stayed in the air for 23 minutes and floated more than five miles.

In 2002, after many unsuccessful attempts, Steve Fossett became the first person ever to travel solo around the world in a balloon. The voyage took the American balloonist 13 days. Carried by air currents and moving only by the power of wind, the balloon traveled between 20 and 200 miles per hour.

Steve Fossett's balloon floats 4 miles above South Africa on June 30, 2002.

Working with the Wind

Like sailboats, windmills use sails to catch the wind's power. They use that power to do work. In windy places, windmills use wind power to grind grain or to pump water.

The first windmills were probably built more than 1,300 years ago. Cloth sails were attached to a large wheel that could spin around on a long pole, or shaft. The sails caught the wind and set the shaft spinning. Inside the mill, a grindstone connected to the shaft turned and ground grain into flour.

Farmers on the Greek island of Crete used windmills to pump water for their crops and livestock. Some of these windmills are still used today.

The Dutch used the power of windmills to help build their country. Much of the land in Holland (now called the Netherlands) was marshy and often flooded by the sea. Windmills helped the Dutch change their land.

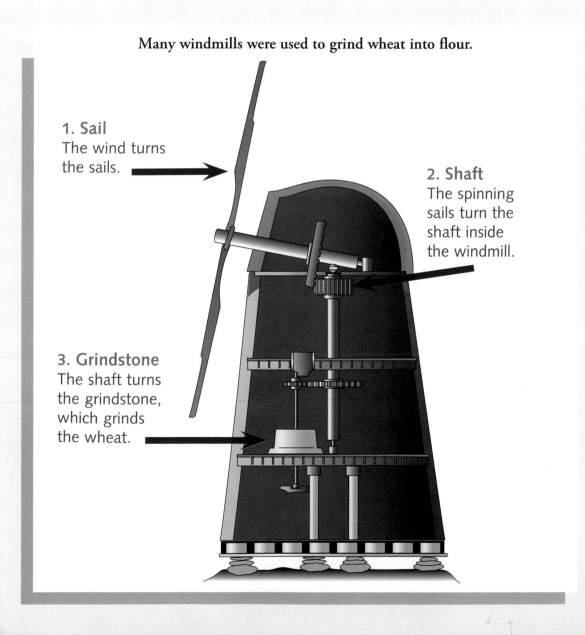

Many windmills were used to grind wheat into flour.

1. Sail
The wind turns the sails.

2. Shaft
The spinning sails turn the shaft inside the windmill.

3. Grindstone
The shaft turns the grindstone, which grinds the wheat.

In the 1800s, there were more than 9,000 windmills in Holland.

Dutch farmers used windmills to drain patches of land and then pump the water into canals. The water became useful for transportation and other purposes instead of destructive. The Dutch turned the marshland into usable farmland, where they could grow corn and wheat. They also built windmills to grind the corn. To this day, Holland still harnesses wind power.

American Windmills

In the United States, the many-bladed windmill pump is a symbol of the midwestern American farm. Early settlers needed to dig wells for water. Windmills helped solve the problem of pumping water from a deep well up to the surface. The settlers used windmills to power the water pumps. The steady winds of the midwestern plains turned the windmill's blades. That motion and energy was transferred to a pump at the bottom of the windmill tower. The pump drew water up from the well into storage tanks on the ground.

During the 1860s, American companies began manufacturing and selling windmill pumps. Windmills for pumping water were common in the Midwest by the 1870s. Then in the 1930s electric energy became available to pump water. The demand for windmills stopped.

As time goes on, more and more people need more and more electricity. The demand for electricity is great, but the cost of electricity is great too.

Most water-pumping windmills have been abandoned. But new wind-driven machines are now being used to make electricity. Giant wind turbines are appearing on America's windy plains.

In the late 1800s, windmills could be found across the Midwest, from Texas cattle ranches to wheat farms in Nebraska. Today, a new kind of windmill is being used.

Wind Power Today

A wind turbine looks like a gigantic fan. But a wind turbine does not work like a fan. It works in reverse. Instead of using electricity to make wind, a wind turbine uses the wind to make electricity. Wind turbines transform the wind's energy into electricity that lights buildings, runs computers, and provides the power for thousands of other tasks.

All wind turbines have a few basic parts. The three-bladed rotor faces into the wind. The wind turns the rotor blades, spinning a shaft that is connected to a generator. The generator makes electricity. The faster the shaft turns, the more energy is made.

Even if the wind shifts, the rotor at the top of the turbine is designed to move so that it always faces directly into the wind.

A wind turbine is very tall because the wind blows faster higher up. A wind turbine works best when the wind is blowing between 9 and 55 miles per hour.

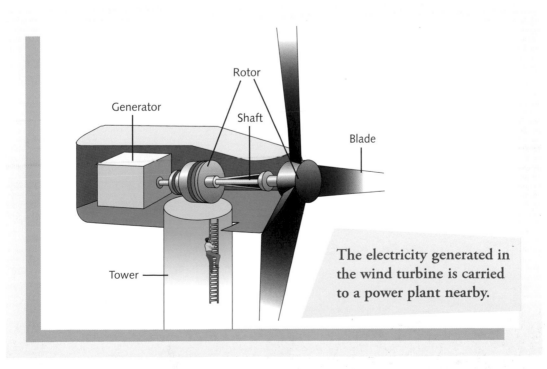

Rotor

Generator

Shaft

Blade

Tower

The electricity generated in the wind turbine is carried to a power plant nearby.

Many wind turbines working together can create as much electricity as a small power plant. A large area of land covered with wind turbines is called a wind farm or a wind plant. A wind farm is a remarkable sight. Imagine acres of 90-meter poles with slow-spinning blades constantly rotating! Each propeller drives a generator.

Can the United States make enough electricity from wind to help supply our country's needs? Some people think so. The United States Department of Energy says there's enough wind in the Great Plains alone to do it!

Today, there are wind farms in California, Colorado, New York, Vermont, and many other places across the country.

Today, there are wind farms in California that generate enough electricity to light up the city of San Francisco. States from New York to Nebraska are also building wind farms to experiment with this source of energy. Even individual homeowners can use the power of wind. In some rural locations, people use a single, small wind turbine to generate electricity.

What ways will people find to use the power of wind in the future?

Somewhere on Earth the wind is blowing. Today it will scatter leaves, carry a boat across the water, and let a bird soar through the sky. Tomorrow, if we want, it can light our homes.

Wind power is energy we can count on. It will always be there. It's ours to use. Like the first sailors, the first fliers, and the first inventors, we need only use our brains to harness the power.

Glossary

aerodynamics: how the shape and design of an object affect how it moves through the air

air currents: the flow of air over land and water

altitude: the height of something above the ground

bow: the front of a boat

engineer: a person trained to use scientific ideas to build things such as airplanes, roads, buildings, and bridges

glider: an aircraft without an engine

goods: things that people make or sell

mast: the tall pole on the deck of a boat that is used to hold the sails

port: a city or town where ships can dock and load or unload their goods

renewable: able to be replaced

rudder: a flat piece of wood or metal that is used to steer a boat

trade winds: the pattern of winds that blow in the same direction toward the equator

wind tunnel: a box or closed structure in which air is blown through; used to test the effects of wind on an object

Index